Shylock of Venice

Shylock of Venice

A Verse Play in Three Acts

by

VICTOR SASSON

iUniverse, Inc.
Bloomington

Shylock Of Venice
A Verse Play in Three Acts

iUniverse books may be ordered through booksellers or by contacting:

iUniverse
1663 Liberty Drive
Bloomington, IN 47403
www.iuniverse.com
1-800-Authors (1-800-288-4677)

Because of the dynamic nature of the Internet, any web addresses or links contained in this book may have changed since publication and may no longer be valid. The views expressed in this work are solely those of the author and do not necessarily reflect the views of the publisher, and the publisher hereby disclaims any responsibility for them.

Any people depicted in stock imagery provided by Thinkstock are models, and such images are being used for illustrative purposes only.
Certain stock imagery © Thinkstock.

ISBN: 978-1-4759-3480-9 (sc)
ISBN: 978-1-4759-3481-6 (ebk)

Printed in the United States of America

iUniverse rev. date: 07/03/2012

BY VICTOR SASSON

Novels:

DESTINED TO DIE

CONFESSIONS OF A SHEEP FOR SLAUGHTER

DR. BUSH AND MR. HIDE

KING JEHOASH AND THE MYSTERY OF THE TEMPLE OF SOLOMON INSCRIPTION

Plays:

THE MARRIAGE OF MAGGIE AND RONNIE

SHYLOCK OF VENICE

Non-Fiction:

ESSAYS FROM OCCUPIED HOLY LAND

MEMOIRS OF A BAGHDAD CHILDHOOD

Poetry—Dramatic Monologues:

CALIBAN ON LANGUAGE

SHYLOCK OUTSIDE COURT

FOREWORD

I must confess I've read *The Merchant* late in my personal career. I knew about the play, of course, and although I had read some of the major tragedies when I was much younger, I skipped this one. Like most people I was impressed with the popular 'quality of mercy' speech and the enchanting (but later, to this writer, detestable) Portia. If at one time I read or skimmed through the play, I tended to stop at the end of the trial scene since the rest of the play seemed to me childish, banal, coming soon after humiliating and practically lynching a man chiefly on account of his religion and ethnicity.

There is no doubt in my mind that *The Merchant* is an anti-Semitic play. But I do not think or believe that Shakespeare himself was anti Jewish. Jews were probably an abstraction for him because it is well known that there were only a handful of Jews in England at the time. Yet he drew a picture of a man, Shylock, who is alive, moving, feeling, believing, outraged and paining in a hostile environment.

Shakespeare was a dramatist. He had to put himself in the shoes of Shylock, as indeed he had to put himself in the shoes of Timon and Lear and Othello. That's what a true dramatist is. A dramatist feels the pain and joy of his characters, especially the major characters in his plays. Nevertheless, something is out of place, definitely incongruent, in his play. The language is mostly elevated language with classical and biblical allusions requiring a highly educated person to understand and appreciate. The trial scene, on the other hand, is designed for the riffraff. It can be understood by anyone, at least superficially.

The whole story of the pound of flesh is a make-believe fantasy, devoid of sense. It was no doubt aimed to entertain the cruder passions of Catholic Christians, but I do not see how an educated person, of whatever religion, would be entertained by the nonsense of the trial. It is a primitive trial scene, unrealistic, crude, and unbelievable. The wooing and romantic scenes of the men and women in the play border on the ridiculous.

The 'quality of mercy' sermon is impressive on its own—but is absolutely *fake within the reality of the play*, for its clear intention is not the exercise of mercy but mere propaganda for Christianity, a religion utterly rejected by the Jewish people. In this sermon Portia is posturing as a devout person when in fact she is quite manipulative, devious, and heartless in her extreme cruelty.

More recently, having seen a cinematic portrayal of Shylock, and my own rejection of Christianity's claims to be based on the Hebrew Bible, I decided to write a play to demolish Portia (as mercifully as possible), expose Christianity and the graven image it worships, and address some other issues. I wanted the trial scene to be more realistic, more down to earth and credible. I wanted to expose Portia and Nerissa as impostors, and their male lovers as bankrupts and idlers—as indeed they appear to be so in Shakespeare's play. I thought Portia and Co. deserved to be dragged down from the pinnacle of Belmont make-believe, for that kind of idealized romance, based on good looks and money, is bound to collapse and disintegrate, sooner rather than later. Bassanio, let us remember was a bankrupt;

Gratiano, dissolute; and Lorenzo, a thief. Certainly I wanted Shylock to have his day in court—and to win. To win, but not necessarily by having a pound of flesh from the despicable Catholic Christian, Antonio, but through other more logical, more realistic and legal, means. Shylock, after all, had a very good cause for retaliation—*within the reality of the play*. In the play and its realities, Shylock is living among nasty, hypocritical and mean Christians who shut him up at night in his Jewish ghetto, spit at him and mock his faith and his profession—day in, day out. He does not come to court because of these and other personal miseries only but also because of the accumulated weight of centuries of abuse heaped on European Jewry for rejecting a supposedly *Jewish* saviour.

Some commentators have said that Shakespeare's play is about Mercy *v.* Law. I reject this. Anyone who can read the Hebrew Bible in Hebrew or in English will see that mercy is a thoroughly Jewish concept—a Middle Eastern concept since the Hebrew Bible was composed and compiled in Palestine and in Babylonia (modern Iraq) by Middle Eastern Jewish prophets and scribes. The concept of mercy is prominent in Jewish liturgy and daily prayers. Mercy in fact has become a corner stone not only of the Jewish faith but also of Islam. To Christian Europe, however, the Jew has become an eyesore because he is a living proof that Jesus is not the Jewish Messiah. Shylock is not hated because of the interest he charges or the revenge he seeks but because he is a living negation of Christianity and its worshipped idol. To wish him away, they speak of the Jew and treat him as sub-human, or refer to him as the devil—and this is quite clear in Shakespeare's play. This is the *ultimate Christian revenge* on the Jew for rejecting Christianity.

Shakespeare blundered when he made Shylock quote the so called 'new' testament. The vast majority of Jews do not read Christian writings. As to Shylock saying he was content upon being forced to convert to Christianity, this is sheer Christian wishful thinking. A resolute and observant Jew, Shylock would never succumb to this kind of religious blackmail.

Regarding Shakespeare's *use* of blank verse, I do not think it is different from that of other Elizabethan dramatists. He was just a much better poet and dramatist. Now although he generally conforms to iambic metre, it was nigh impossible for him—as indeed for any other poet—to stick to it, simply because natural speech in poetic drama cannot bear strict adherence to rules. He has regular and irregular lines, lines that are twelve or thirteen syllables, lines that end even with a preposition such as 'at', and various artificial elisions. In my play I have tried to write verse that can be spoken and recited naturally, even sometimes at the expense of violating iambic rule and its stress pattern. I don't think this is much different from Shakespeare's practice, those of his contemporaries, and the verse of Webster and Ford. It remains to be seen whether the verse in this play is effective or not.

The actual writing of this play took some two months, from mid-June to mid-August. While the play still unpublished, I took the time to look at the verse again and correct oversights and delete and add some dialogue, particularly in the trial scene. The additions amounted to some four pages in the present book format. The structure of the play, however, remained the same. I have retained the original date of the play's completion.

V. S.
August 2011

The Actors in the Play

The Duke of Venice
State Senators
Professor Victor Sassoon a *literary sleuth and private detective*
Dr. Simon Watkins *his colleague and assistant*
Shylock *a Jewish moneylender/banker*
Jessica *his daughter*
Tubal *his Jewish friend*
Portia *a rich heiress, later impersonating a Dr. Balthazar*
Nerissa *her former maid, later impersonating a lawyer's clerk*
Antonio *a Christian merchant*
Bassanio *his close friend, married to Portia*
Gratiano *friend to Antonio and Bassanio, married to Nerissa*
Lorenzo *friend to Antonio and Bassanio, married to Jessica*
Prince of Morocco and Prince of Arragon *formerly suitors to Portia*
Launcelot *a clown, servant to Bassanio; formerly servant to Shylock*
Court Clerk
A Moorish Girl *holding an infant*
Her Moorish Parents and Relatives
Citizens, Guards, Attendants, Messengers

ACT ONE

Scene 1

London.

Professor Sassoon's residence at 317c Maida Vale.
Sassoon is holding an unopened letter. The door bell rings.
At the door is Dr. Simon Watkins, his friend and colleague.

SASSOON
Ah, you have come in good time. Take a look at this.

WATKINS
It's a letter.

SASSOON
Good deduction, Watkins. Examine it closely.

WATKINS
By the stamp, it is a letter from Venice.

SASSOON
Venice, of all places. I get letters from far and near but this
is the first time there's one from Venice.

WATKINS

Consider it a blessing. You are always in demand to solve some mystery, to save some neck or other. Why don't you open it and see what's it's all about? It could be, you know, an invitation from the Duke of Venice for a ball, some festivity, some bull-fighting event . . .

SASSOON

My dear fellow, there is no such thing as bull fighting in Venice. It is half-covered by water. And the Duke of Venice is the last person on earth to send me an invitation of any kind. Here, open it and read it for me. I dread what it says as I have no inclination now to venture overseas, even to save a neck from hanging or a head from beheading.

WATKINS [Opens the letter and reads.]

Dear Professor Sassoon,

My community in Venice, whose head I myself represent, has heard about your exploits in solving crimes of every sort and defending the weak against evil individuals and government abuses.

I am writing on behalf of my good friend, Shylock, who has been wrongfully indicted and sentenced in a most bizarre and fraudulent way. This is a legal case that has shocked and rocked our small and vulnerable Jewish community here. We have come together to try to reclaim our dear Shylock. The full details of the case will be known to you upon your coming to Venice to investigate this tragedy and, if possible, to reopen his court case. You have

our community's assurance that all expenses of travel and
lodging will be reimbursed.

On behalf of the Jewish community of Venice, I am, Sir,

Your most humble Servant,
Tubal of Venice

It seems you are desperately needed, Professor. Will you go?

SASSOON
Watkins, the world's awash with injustices.
Shall I engage in globe-trotting at every
Desperate call for help? Shall I set right
What crookedness has crookedly devised?
Am I the moral arm of an immoral world?
Can there be a shortage of legal pundits
And detectives in Venice that calls for
A foreigner to be imported from London?

WATKINS
You're too humble, Sassoon. This letter proves
You have gained a reputation abroad,
A name that carries with it some measure of
Responsibility. I don't see how you can
Ignore this cry for help which sounds so urgent.

SASSOON
Fiddlesticks, Watkins. Cries for help are ever
Urgent and demanding. But let me think it over.
This missive does speak, nay, cries for redress.
And may deserve a hearing and perhaps
Even a venture to far-away Venice.

3

WATKINS
A whole community looks up to you
For help. To them, you are a light that can
Brighten their lives by reclaiming this Shylock,
Whoever he is and whatever he has done.
Since you found it fit to go to Jerusalem
To solve the mystery of King Solomon's tablet,
This case, too, appears to be of equal,
If not more than equal importance.

SASSOON
I've heard you, loud and clear, Watkins.
Let me consult my schedule, and do same
With yours, and if we are unfettered
With other responsibilities, we shall
Undertake this venture and consider it
A kind of vacation, a paid holiday.

WATKINS
Very well put, Professor. Let's do that.

SASSOON
And having succeeded in our mission,
We can stop by Spain and watch a bullfight.

WATKINS
Capital!
Now how do you propose we go to Venice?
Shall we fly, take a boat, or go by land?
What's your preference?

SASSOON
            To fly if we can get wings.

But first draft a letter to this Tubal
And apprise him of our consent to his plea,
And demand details regarding an appeal
To the court of Venice to reopen
This Shylock's case.

WATKINS
Consider it done.

> *Exeunt* Sassoon and Watkins.

> *

Scene 2

Venice.

Shylock's mean lodging outside the ghetto.

> *Enter* Shylock and Tubal.

SHYLOCK
Woe is me for this life, Tubal. I am destitute and sick at
heart. Look at this mean lodging and see my poor health.
This plight has added years to my life. I reckon I am older
by ten years. I'll die a poor man, not a penny to my name.
My house is gone, my wealth is gone, all is gone . . .

TUBAL
But not your faith. You are still the son of our father,
Abraham. You must have hope, you must have patience.

SHYLOCK

Yes, I need patience. I need the patience of Job, but I am no Job. I am a moneylender, a banker, a businessman, but now without a business to speak of. It's not enough that my house and my wealth have been snatched away from me by Christian wolves but I have been forced into their sham religion and must bend my knees to their crucified idol.

TUBAL

Do it in show only, as they too do it in show only, for their faith is naught; it is null and void in the sight of God. They are good at preaching love but they have no love. They treat us, badly, like animals, locking us up in a ghetto at night. You see, we are a thorn in their side because we don't accept their graven image, which they call messiah, as though we Jews are too stupid to recognize our own true Messiah when he comes. Never despair of retribution to fall on enemies of the truth. Shylock, you have been steadfast in your love for your departed wife, Lea; steadfast in your faith, steadfast in the Covenant, and right in demanding the fulfilment of the bond.

SHYLOCK

Yes, yes, the bond which was dearly bought by me. I wanted to see the fall of Antonio, who, hating and cursing our chosen seed, oftentimes spat on me and called me cutthroat dog.

TUBAL

By spitting on us, Jews, they but spit on their god, for their god was a Jew, born out of wedlock, but they claim he came about by some holy ghost. But we think his mother was a punk, and being burdened with an unwanted child, blamed God for it.

SHYLOCK
Belike, a ghost story, or more likely, a ghastly story.

TUBAL
And if you believe that story, you can believe anything.
Now listen, Shylock . . .

SHYLOCK
What? I feel you have some good news for me. I see it in
your eyes. Come, what is it?

TUBAL
Shylock, our Jewish community prays for you. You are
always in our prayers. We have come together to try to
reverse your fortunes; to deliver you, if we can. We've
written to a man in London, a literary sleuth and smart
detective, well-known for his acumen in solving criminal
and legal knots. We have asked him to help us reopen your
case . . .

SHYLOCK
But how? How? I do not understand, Tubal.

TUBAL
We claim your trial was a sham since Balthazar was no
lawyer. It was a wealthy woman of Belmont called Portia
who played the masked thief.

SHYLOCK
She was! I knew it! I knew it, all along. A fraud, a cheat!
A Christian cheat, clothed in the mantle of our prophet,
Daniel.

TUBAL
We live a precarious life, Shylock, being Jews in a Christian country.

SHYLOCK
I know, I know. But good news, Tubal; good news! Oh, I am so glad, so glad. You've poured some cold water over my singed and anguished heart.

TUBAL
Have heart, Shylock. We are working on this matter. We will get results, God willing. What news of your daughter, Jessica?

SHYLOCK
Talk not of her. The whore! She is not my daughter anymore than a dog in the streets of Venice or a jackal in the hills.

TUBAL
But she might repent, Shylock. She might yet repent and come back to our fold and to your fatherly embrace. She is bound to see the trickeries of these Christians and the hollowness of their faith. We have had such infatuations before in our community. Young blood is too hot, too tempestuous, and often errs. Who doesn't fall in love at sixteen and seventeen, Shylock?

SHYLOCK
No, Tubal. She was born a whorish slut. Exchanged my wife Leah's turquoise ring for a monkey! She has made a monkey of me. She has made a monkey of me, I tell you.

TUBAL

She has made a monkey of our Jewish community but, Shylock, we cannot despair.

SHYLOCK

I wouldn't have exchanged that ring she stole for a wilderness of monkeys. It tortures me to think about it, Tubal.

TUBAL

The day will come when you can buy a better turquoise ring in memory of your wife.

SHYLOCK

Yes, yes, but not that ring . . . unless we can somehow get hold of it again. Purchase it, I mean to say.

TUBAL

Here, Shylock, read the book of Psalms. I brought you a copy of this holy book. In it you read how the mighty are brought low, and the despised are raised up from the dungeon. (*Hands him the book*).

SHYLOCK

I have a copy of our holy Hebrew Bible, but this small book will be my companion. You have revived my soul, Tubal, with your good news. I shall recite and study these psalms every day.

TUBAL

Do so, good Shylock. And I shall apprise you of any new news I get from our good man in London.

SHYLOCK
May God be with you in this matter.

TUBAL
Amen! Don't forget to read the Psalms of David. Fare thee well.

SHYLOCK
I will, I will, good Tubal.

Exeunt Shylock and Tubal.

*

Scene 3

A Street in Venice.

Enter Launcelot and Lorenzo.

LAUNCELOT
Good morning, sir Lorenzo.

LORENZO
Good morning.

LAUNCELOT
Sir, you look sad and that doesn't become you, a married man of scarcely one year old marriage. Truly, I do hope you and your wife are in good health and thriving.

LORENZO
The devil take her! He may have her as his wife.

LAUNCELOT
The devil? That's no way to talk about your wife. What's the matter?

LORENZO
Three things she refuses to eat.

LAUNCELOT
What can these be, sir Lorenzo.

LORENZO
Pork, ham, and bacon.

LAUNCELOT
But these are our Holy Trinity by which we Christians swear. Is she recanting, is she turning Jew again? Oh sir, what a mess! Refusing to eat pork! Mark me, she is still a Jew. For, sir, a Jew is a Jew and cannot be mended. It is someone whose nature refuses to be mended.

LORENZO
She claims her father, Shylock, had from childhood forbidden her even to smell pork, let alone taste it, and that she cannot now, after all those years, convert to eating it.

LAUNCELOT
Then she hasn't converted to our religion yet. She will shame you, left and right, for how can you celebrate Christmas and Easter and family gatherings without a slaughter of pigs?

LORENZO
There's only myself to blame, Launcelot.

LAUNCELOT
Make sure you get no issue from her, for the child will be a half Jew. And if they be twins, you will be twice devilled.

LORENZO
Good advice from one who has pumped up the belly of the Moorish servant.

LAUNCELOT
The girl was asking for it, sir. Don't put the whole blame on me. She was asking for it.

LORENZO
The usual excuse a bawd has up his sleeve for impregnating a wench.

LAUNCELOT
But, sir, the issue will be a blessing for us as it will be more than half a Christian, and less than half a Mohammedan.

LORENZO
You are evading the issue for your head would've been chopped off had Bassanio, Gratiano, and I myself not intervened with her incensed relatives.

LAUNCELOT
For which I have thanked you all a million times.

LORENZO
Not enough times.

LAUNCELOT
But you too are dodging the issue, sir. Is Jessica with child?

LORENZO
We lack evidence as yet of an issue from her, but I do
pray daily she is not with child and that would put an end
to the issue.

Enter Jessica.

How now, where are you running to? A new lover?

JESSICA
Take your hand off me!

LORENZO
One year married and you've turned shrew. Look, Launcelot,
this is the woman I've taken for a wife. Take a good look at
her.

JESSICA
You are hurting me. Launcelot, speak to him.

LAUNCELOT
Not until he bids me speak.

JESSICA
You are not the Launcelot I once knew.

LAUNCELOT
And you are not the Jessica I once knew.

JESSICA
Let go off me!

LORENZO
Not until you tell me where you are running to.

JESSICA
To see my father after all these months.

LORENZO
To see Shylock? Is he still your father, traitor? What has come to you; why is this change?

JESSICA
You are a drunkard, a good for nothing husband. I have squandered my father's jewels and ducats, which would be mine someday by natural inheritance, and you have not supported me. You are like your friends who are a pack of idlers and foul-mouthed parrots. Let go off me!

LORENZO
Shall I break her arm, Launcelot? She calls me drunkard, an idler, and a parrot.

LAUNCELOT
A parrot? A parrot has no brains and you are a gentleman with a head on your shoulders.

JESSICA
A gentleman with brains doesn't lounge about all day, play cards, throw dice, get drunk, and swear all the time. And half the time you are not home, spending your time in the fantasy land of Belmont.

LORENZO
Look, how this big spender talks.

JESSICA
Those were moments of insanity. I was not myself. Passion drove me to excess.

LAUNCELOT
Now she is the repentant sinner. In a wink I'll start crying. Hand me a handkerchief, sir.

LORENZO
Don't blame your dissolution on insanity. Your passion was burning hot under and over the bed sheets.

LAUNCELOT
She cannot be mended. She is a mix of false Christian and faithless Jew. Send her away. Get rid of her.

[Lorenzo releases her arm.]

LORENZO
Go! But I expect a pork chop for supper this evening, or else I'll chop off your hands?

JESSICA
But please, sir, have mercy on me, have mercy on me! Show Christian mercy!

LAUNCELOT
She is mocking you, Lorenzo, with her tongue out, too.

Exit Jessica, running.

What will you do now, sir? She has proved to be faithless like the Jew her father.

LORENZO
I'll do nothing as I still dote on her. I cannot help it.

LAUNCELOT
Then, with your permission, sir, you are drunk. You will get sober when you get rid of her.

LORENZO
For a fool and a clown, sirrah, you speak words of wisdom.

LAUNCELOT
Your words, sir, speak highly of me, undeservedly. Fare you well. There is a pub nearby where you can drown your sorrow, but drown nothing else.

LORENZO
Get thee hence before I try my sharp sword on you.

LAUNCELOT
No offence intended, sir.

Exit Lorenzo.

As to pumping up the Moor's belly, it was great fun, more than she deserved. It was a piece of Christian charity on my part. Her folks are foreign workers, aliens, cheap labour, and have no say in the matter. I have nothing to worry about. Let her give the child for adoption—for mercy's sake.

Enter Jessica.

JESSICA

You still speak of mercy, you unmerciful piece of Christian scum. Mercy is a Jewish word—so the rabbi at the synagogue told me and showed it to me in our Hebrew Scripture.

LAUNCELOT

What, why are you back so soon from seeing your father?

JESSICA

He wouldn't open the door for me. He calls me whore. He also says I've been defiled by the uncircumcised Christians.

LAUNCELOT

The sins of the fathers are visited upon their children. I've told you that before.

JESSICA

The devil can quote our Hebrew Scripture to suit his purpose.

LAUNCELOT

You call me devil, you that handled my devilled private parts before marrying Lorenzo.

JESSICA

Lecher! Devil of a lecher! You got me into corners even after my marriage to Lorenzo.

LAUNCELOT

But you were a willing victim. Your vagina was aching for that one pound of solid flesh, which I gave it to you gratis. You sucked it in with relish and anguish. Like the young Moor, you craved it. You were asking for it, weren't you?

JESSICA
Lecher! Lecher! Lecher!

LAUNCELOT
Let's go to church and repent us of our sins. You will embrace your Christian faith and I will renounce lechery.

JESSICA
Ha! Ha! Ha! What a clown you are! I will repent me of being a Christian. I shall be tutored in my ancient faith. There will be Jewish mercy for me. It is all written in our Hebrew Bible, the rabbi tells me.

LAUNCELOT
No, as a Jew, there is no mercy for you in heaven. As for me, Jesus will forgive my lechery as I know he was a lecher himself, and so I'll be saved from hell.

JESSICA
No, you are damned, damned. You played tricks even on your half-blind father. That's what Christian charity is.

LAUNCELOT
What about you, thieving from your father?

JESSICA
It was Lorenzo who pressed me to thieve. He not only stole me from my father, but also made me rob him of my mother's ring, and his ducats and jewels. I was a hardened fool, in love, half blind.

LAUNCELOT
Blaming it on blind love? No. You are a born whore.

Exeunt separately.

*

Scene 4

Sassoon's flat in London.

Enter Sassoon and Watkins.

WATKINS
What news from Tubal? What has transpired
Since last I saw you? Come, I am all ears.

SASSOON
A most bizarre story, Watkins, deserving
Of our attention and may merit further
Investigation and a necessary
Venture to Venice.

WATKINS
        Go on, Professor.
Since you speak with such enthusiasm,
The tale must be tantalizing indeed.

SASSOON
Here are the outlines: in Belmont there is
A lady whose late father had left her
A huge fortune with a strange stipulation
Of lottery by caskets and inscriptions
So as to test and win the wisest husband
For his daughter, whose name is Portia.

Bassanio, a spendthrift and a bankrupt,
Sought to woo this lady, but lacking funds,
Turned to his friend, Antonio, a merchant,
For instant cash, to make a show of wealth,
And compete with wealthy and titled suitors.
Antonio, a risk-taker, had all his fortune
In goods tossing upon the high seas.
Bassanio, distrusted by fellow Christians,
Turned to Shylock, a Jewish moneylender,
To lend three thousand ducats for three months,
With merchant Antonio as guarantor.
Since this Christian merchant had much abused
And reviled Shylock for being both Jew
And moneylender who charged interest,
This Shylock had nothing but brewing hatred
For Antonio, yet agreed to disburse
The full three thousand ducats for three months—
Without charging interest. But hear this:
There was a strange condition that a pound
Of flesh would be cut from this Antonio,
Upon forfeiture of the bond.

WATKINS
Ha! Ha! Ha! A pound of flesh!

SASSOON
            That's correct.
It was meant at first to be just a joke
But turned deadly as events unfolded.
A bond was signed and sealed by a notary,
With Antonio's pledge that Shylock could exact
The full penalty should he default.

WATKINS
Then he's a fool of a merchant.

SASSOON
Definitely, and most probably suicidal,
Like the Nazarene image he worships.
His ships were reported wrecked while the bond
Had matured. Shylock would accept no money,
Insisting on fulfilment of the bond.
In court, he was left to fend for himself,
With this wolf, Portia, preaching a fine sermon
On the quality of mercy while scheming
To tear him to pieces and then lynch him.

WATKINS
A woman preaching, Samuel Johnson said,
Is like a dog walking on his hind legs.
Although not done well, you are surprised
To find it done at all.

SASSOON
          Excellent, Watkins.
Through legal trickeries and ancient hatred,
All was tailored to turn out well for Christians,
But horribly disastrous for the Jew.
The Christian was painted a pure angel,
The Jew, the devil incarnate.

WATKINS
Shylock is depicted as a typical Jew.

SASSOON
Quite so! The Jews had for thousands of years

Been the butt of Christian malice for rejecting
Jesus as their long-awaited Messiah.

WATKINS
I know. Don't forget my field is history.
But there is something quite weird in the story.
What kind of friendship exists between
Antonio and his loyal friend Bassanio?
To risk a gruesome death to save a debtor
Poses some serious questions to my mind.
Don't you think?

SASSOON
    Definitely, my dear fellow.
I need data to determine the kind
Of love and loyalty involved. Suffice it
To say it doesn't look legit to both of us.

WATKINS
What's next, Professor?

SASSOON
Since I assumed Tubal would not succeed
In his efforts to reopen Shylock's case,
I've sent an urgent missive to our British
Ambassador in Venice to put pressure
On the Duke to consider a retrial.

WATKINS
What kind of pressure could the man exert?

SASSOON
Economic pressure is the best tool.

Trade involves prosperity and wealth,
And the Venetians, having business acumen,
Are sensitive to punitive sanctions.

WATKINS
Do you think this will work?

SASSOON
       It's worth a try.
Venice is at centre of international trade
And its reputation lies in its dealings
Both with its citizens and its aliens.
A nasty name in trade, my dear Watkins,
Is a death warrant to any businessman
Or country. It is shunned like a plague.

WATKINS
You've met the man, I suppose.

SASSOON
       Once or twice,
Here in England and on the continent,
In my local and foreign adventures.
Dudley Carleton is a shrewd fellow.

WATKINS
Let's hope your plans work.

SASSOON
Amen!

            Exeunt Sassoon and Watkins.

ACT TWO

Scene 1

A bedroom in Portia's house in Belmont.

Enter Portia and Bassanio.

PORTIA
Scarcely a year passed and you've squandered
Three quarters of my fortune. My good father
Would have died of sorrow and despair
To see that I've chosen a confirmed gambler.
At the contest, you said nothing about
The casket you picked because we told you
Which one to choose. You brooded on verse
I myself provided to fool those present.
No, no. A man with your miniscule brain
Would never have guessed the right inscription.
And now you are impoverishing me;
In no time I shall end up a vagabond.

BASSANIO
Nay, but let me speak a word or two.
I've made bets that turned out to be toxic.
I've embarked on schemes and promising plans
That did not materialize. The fault is not

24

Mine alone. But I do bear responsibility.
I own that much and I confess that much.

PORTIA
By heaven it is much too much to own.
You're a gambler and have always been broke.
You have lived lavishly, beyond your means.
You squandered your own fortune, borrowed
Three thousand ducats from Shylock, with Antonio
Hostage to your whims, protested love to me
When all your honeyed words were mere wind.
I fell in love with you, not knowing you were
A nothing, with nothing but good looks
And a brain that's as void as it is hollow.
You would never have chosen the right casket
Had not Nerissa, at my command, told you.
You would have chosen the most obvious one:
'Who chooseth me shall have as much as he deserves'.
And you would have left with two fool's heads—
One in hand, and that one on your shoulders.

BASSANIO
Go on, mock me; tear me to pieces, I
Deserve every word and insult you hurl
At me. Let me be the aim of your fury
And the butt of your jokes, jibes, and ridicule.
I submit I'm a fool, and I own I am
A gambler by nature and, as Shylock
Had put it, I am 'the prodigal Christian'—
So Launcelot, my servant, has relayed.
I am a compulsive gambler, Portia,
With cards, casinos and roulettes for ever
Spinning in my giddy, empty head.

I aim for the stars but I often find
My feet stuck on the ground, mired in debts,
And many a time Antonio has saved me
From the dungeon of embezzlers and crooks.

PORTIA
I know that much, Bassanio. But, come, tell,
Confess your true motives for our sham marriage.
Speak, don't hold up. Confess, confess!

BASSANIO
I do confess I've loved thee for your money.
Your coffers seemed quite inexhaustible,
Irresistible, beckoning, alluring,
Rather sinful for one person to possess.
But I've made you rich with the love you craved,
And you have made me rich with your coffers.

PORTIA
Get out of my house, you rotten dissembler
And counterfeit lover! You've broken my heart
But I will not let you break my coffers,
Or I shall roam the streets in rags, a pauper
Begging for a morsel of bread, homeless,
In public parks, sleeping on cardboards.
I'll end up my days as a working girl
Tempting clients in dark alleys of Venice.
Get out of my house! Go, go, go!

BASSANIO
Is this your quality of mercy, Portia?
Is this what you have been preaching to Jews?

Why don't you practise what you preach?
Your sermons are worthless, not worth a penny.
They're all empty words, lacking any value.
Come, show me some of that mercy you preached,
Or I'll go to Jews to have a taste of it.

PORTIA
There's no mercy for embezzlers and crooks.
Neither Jews nor Christians can give it to you.

BASSANIO
Look who's talking! You've deceived our Duke.
You made a monkey of him, fooling him,
Pretending to be Doctor Bellario.
You would be hanged in no time for this crime
And, if pressured, I could inform on you.
So take note of my warning. I am serious.
Don't stretch your luck too much.

PORTIA
        Inform on me?
You, vile wretch, you bastard, son of a bitch!
You, whom I have rescued out of the gutters
Of debts and broken bonds! You, you!
Trickster, embezzler, counterfeit lover!
                        [Sobbing.]

BASSANIO
Call me what you will. This is *my* house.
And if you don't like it, there is the door.

               Exeunt Portia and Bassanio.

*

Scene 2

A yard in Gratiano's house.

Enter Launcelot and Gratiano.

LAUNCELOT
My lord Bassanio sent me to tell you he cannot meet you this evening.

GRATIANO
What's his reason; did he give any reason? We had agreed to meet as usual, to party with our friend, Lorenzo.

LAUNCELOT
His wife is giving him a hard time and, if I may say so, a drabbing for partying every other night of the week.

GRATIANO
This is our new age when women seek to take over the sceptre of lordship from their husbands. Go, tell your master never to fear but to let the fear of the husband be upon the wife. And if she be disobedient and obdurate, he must have the will to chase her out of the house.

LAUNCELOT
If I may say so, sir, the house belongs to her.

GRATIANO
Fool, she had already given half the house to him; and the other half is his as a legal partner in a legal marriage.

LAUNCELOT
But was it lawful to do so, sir?

GRATIANO
It was both lawful and legal. It was lawful because she had the right to do it, and legal because it is enforceable in the eyes of the law.

LAUNCELOT
So Portia now is homeless, without a house.

GRATIANO
That's correct. She is now a guest in Bassanio's mansion, under his protection. Go, tell your master he is not to be dictated to by his wife. The Devil take her! She has turned dictator. That's what happens to women after they get a husband. What else is there to do in life if not partying every other night? What's the point of having so much money and property, if not to throw it about and enjoy it before old age and white hair.

LAUNCELOT
Shall I tell him all of this?

GRATIANO
Just tell him I say he is the lord and master of his house and his wife must be obedient and subservient. And tell him we shall party tomorrow instead of today.

LAUNCELOT
Most obediently, sir.

GRATIANO
Why don't you go? What is it?

LAUNCELOT
Sir, I am about to lose my job with Bassanio who had hired me. Since Portia now pays my wages, I fear I shall lose my service. She has this morning dismissed two of her maids.

GRATIANO
Is that so?

LAUNCELOT
Her fortune, sir, is being drained by my master, the Christian prodigal. And he has been neglecting his wife, if you receive my meaning. I could hear her sobbing at night when she craves his company and he is away with his Antonio.

GRATIANO
What do you mean by 'his Antonio'?

LAUNCELOT
If you don't mind me saying so, sir, Antonio is his lover.

GRATIANO
His lover? How come you know of this, sirrah. Speak!

LAUNCELOT
A servant has more than two ears, sir. We hear voices all the time, and see things, too.

GRATIANO
No wonder Shylock recommended you to Bassanio. You must be insane.

LAUNCELOT
I try not to be so, sir.

GRATIANO
So forget what you hear and close your eyes to what you see.

LAUNCELOT
But it is against God's law for a man to copulate with another man. My former master, the devil Shylock, expounded the Law of Moses to me. It is an abomination for a man to sleep with another man.

GRATIANO
Fool, that law is already outdated. The new law has allowed it.

LAUNCELOT
You are right, sir. I forgot Jesus had twelve men as gay fornicators.

GRATIANO
Very well put. For a fool and a servant, you know your Bible well.

LAUNCELOT
I learned my Bible from Shylock. He said Christians are fornicators and idolaters for they worship a dead Jew, meaning, Yeshu, yet we Christians hate Jews.

GRATIANO
He wouldn't dare talk about Christians in public for he would be lynched.

LAUNCELOT
He has been lynched a couple of times in the past, and he deserves lynching again, just for the fun of it. He is an alien just like the servant Moor and has no rights.

GRATIANO
I hear Nerissa calling. Go now and tell Bassanio we shall party with Lorenzo tomorrow.

Exit Gratiano.

LAUNCELOT
In a flash, sir.

One piece of damning news I held myself from telling this buffoon is that Portia had fooled not only our Duke of Venice by impersonating Doctor Bellario but that she also deceived the two princes, the rich suitors that sought her hand in marriage. Launcelot, I say to myself, there is a fortune to be made here, some hundreds of ducats or Spanish dinars or Moroccan gold coins. Information is worth its weight in gold. Intelligence may lead to conquest of nations, and of individuals. Once rich, I'll dress up like a vizier, like a high quality prince myself, impersonate a duke or something. And, indeed, why not? Aren't we all born equal? In truth, I've heard some wise philocipher, or maybe Shylock himself, saying we are created in the image of God. Imagine me, widely considered a fool, to have been created by God himself. I mean, deflect for a moment, God himself took the trouble to fashion a humble person like me, a mere nothing, a nonentity, a very minor screw in the scheme of universal things. What have you to say about this, Launcelot? And why can I not dress up like a prince, a Prince of Netherland, or Nottingham, or Nothing, if there is a place called Nothing or Notting. And so I will send a missile, meaning an urgent missive, to these two princes deluding to them that they have been fooled by this sweetly poisonous Portia, this lady of baloney Belmont. And, if my gut feeling be correct, I could extradicate some good amount of funds from them by way of Christian charity, to set things aright. In truth, I need to do this since I am now about to lose my service with the household of Portia and Bassanio, and most likely to be cast out into the gutters and sewage canals of Venice.

Exit Launcelot.

*

Scene 3

A bedroom in Gratiano's house.

Enter Nerissa and Gratiano.

NERISSA
Our house is hell and it's you who make it so.
You gamble, you drink, carouse and chatter
All day, talking rubbish with Bassanio
And Lorenzo. And you treat me, your wife,
With gross disrespect. One year of marriage
And we are worlds apart. We are now strangers.

I don't know you at all. You are wild, crude,
And rude. I want you out, out of my life.
You're not the man I married.

GRATIANO
Your complaints are common complaints of wives.
It's boredom that's making you disgruntled.
Your mind craves employment and your hands, work.
Keep busy, manage the house, scrub the floors,
Wash the dishes, do laundry, and keep silent.
Remember: I am your lord and master.

NERISSA
Oh, what a monster you have become!
Bassanio was right saying you excel
In talking nonsense. I am not your servant.
I'm your lawfully wedded wife, your partner
In life, but I've no more wish to be so.
Our house is home to mice, our beds, to lice.
We have no servants and you lend no hand
To the upkeep of the house.

GRATIANO
        Go back to Portia.

NERISSA
Portia is no more the mistress of her house,
And I am no more her maid. We parted
With tears for Bassanio has squandered much
Of her huge fortune, and you know it.
He has been supporting you and Lorenzo.
He has been feeding you with Portia's ducats.

GRATIANO
We are loyal friends and share the same pocket.
We love each other dearly and are willing
To die for each other, if necessary.
One for all, and all for one—that's our motto.

NERISSA
Share the same pocket, eh? You have no pocket
To speak of. You are broke, living a life
Of fantasy, of jest and debauchery.
What will you do when Portia's assets vanish?
How will we feed ourselves? Tell me, how?

GRATIANO
We will beg for food or go to Utopia
Where assets are fit for asses to carry;
Where food and shelter are never needed.

NERISSA
Ever the daydreamer, ever the asinine
Make-believer. Come, grow up, be a man!

GRATIANO
How dare you question my manhood, Nerissa!
I am not your child to scold and rebuke.

NERISSA
What has become of your marriage vows? Speak!
Have we come to this?

GRATIANO
            Blame yourself for it.

NERISSA
Oh Shylock! You are having your revenge
At last. The Jew's revenge for fooling him,
For turning him into a monkey.

GRATIANO
And fooling the Duke of Venice, pretending
To be a lawyer's clerk, a fucking male,
Without a penis. I could inform on you.
You would hang for that crime.

NERISSA
      Inform on me?
You scoundrel, you pimp, you son of nobody!

GRATIANO
Ha! Ha! Ha! You need a good beating, that's it.

NERISSA
Wife beater, wife beater! O, woe me!
          [Sobbing.]

      Exeunt Gratiano and Nerissa.

         *

Scene 4

An open yard at Bassanio's house in Belmont.

      Enter Bassanio, then a Messenger.

BASSANIO
Yes?

MESSENGER
I have here a sealed letter from a Venetian merchant called Antonio. I am to deliver it to none other but to his friend, Bassanio.

BASSANIO
I am he.

[Messenger hands the letter to Bassanio.]

Here is a ducat for thee.

Exit Messenger.

BASSANIO (opens the letter and reads)
Sweet Bassanio, I have bad news. My ships and argosies are lost. I had again foolishly ventured all my wealth to the currents and turmoil of the oceans. I have had news of a lost ship only to be followed by news of another lost ship. One to Tripolis was pirated and plundered. Another to Mexico ran against rocks and sank. A third, to the Indies, was lost in a tsunami. I am penniless, broke. This time the news is not mistaken. It is true and has been verified.

> Your loving and loyal friend,
> Antonio

BASSANIO
O sweet Antonio, whatever wealth I have is at your fingertips to use. To Venice must I at once.

Exit Bassanio.

*

Scene 5

Shylock's mean lodging in Venice.

Enter Shylock and Tubal.

SHYLOCK
Welcome, Tubal. What news? Why, you are panting for air.

TUBAL
Good news, Shylock, good news.

SHYLOCK
What, what? Calm down, calm down. You are too excited.

TUBAL
Antonio is ruined . . .

SHYLOCK
What did you say? Antonio ruined? What?

TUBAL
His ships are all destroyed.

SHYLOCK
But . . . but we've had such news before. We had such news before and it turned out to be false rumour. Come now, this is but rumour, nothing more.

TUBAL
Not this time, I tell thee. Our merchant of Venice is a fool, a gambler like the rest of the Christian pack. He risked all his merchandise and wealth to the hazards of the high seas.

SHYLOCK
But is the news verified, Tubal? Is it, is it?

TUBAL
Yes, beyond doubt. It's the talk at the Rialto and elsewhere.

SHYLOCK
Then Shylock, thou hast your revenge at long last! O God of Abram, Lord of Hosts, of the Chariots of Israel. Mark my words, Tubal, this is an Act of God, an Act of God, nothing less. My vow, my oath, has come to pass. By our holy Sabbath, God is repaying our enemies many times for the insults, injuries, and the injustices our nation has suffered. God is exacting more than a pound of Christian flesh.

TUBAL
To feed fish with.

SHYLOCK
Or bait fish withal.

TUBAL
Depend upon it, Shylock, he will either kill himself or go insane—one or the other. We have seen it before here in Venice. Remember?

SHYLOCK

Yes, yes. One went mad, another threw himself into the river, and a third hanged himself. I knew their names—Signior Minelli, Signior Salieri. This one, if I can prophesy, will hang himself, and I'll be glad to offer him a gift of a halter, a ring around his neck.

TUBAL

Let us not exult in the downfall of our enemies. Our Jewish faith does not permit it, and we are cautioned not to do so. Although they deserve punishment, we should not exult in their fall. Remember, Shylock, God had pity on the Egyptians, drowning in the Red Sea.

SHYLOCK

God Almighty, I give thee thanks for this day, for you are the final Arbiter. Antonio is a Jew-hater and a Jew-baiter.

TUBAL

A sodomite, as I have half-heard at the Rialto one day.

SHYLOCK

A sodomite, you say? No wonder, a sodomite, no wonder. He must be one. I did him no wrong yet many a time he spat his venom on me and shamed me in the Rialto, and in the open spaces of Venice. And what's his reason? I am a Jew. Yes, yes, he's a sodomite. That's him; that's Antonio, the Christian pig. Our rabbis of old consigned such a person to hell.

Exeunt Shylock and Tubal.

*

Scene 6

A fashionable resort in Trieste.

Enter Prince of Morocco, and Prince of Arragon
(holding an open letter in his hand).

ARRAGON
This letter from this man Launcelot proves
Both of us have been made blinking idiots
By this woman of Belmont, namely Portia,
Who had led us by the nose to those caskets
Which were so cleverly framed and doctored.

MOROCCO
By Allah, she'll pay for the indignities
We have suffered, honourable Arragon.
In my country, I would cut off her head
And stick it high on a twelve feet pole
For eagles to feed on.

ARRAGON
          In my country
I would hang her, quarter and draw her,
Then burn her on a heap of cow's dung.

MOROCCO,
O what a fool I was to apologize
For my complexion, Prince of Arragon.

ARRAGON
How? What is it you said, Prince of Morocco?

MOROCCO
'Mistake me not for my complexion.'

ARRAGON
How could she mistake you, Prince of Morocco?
Your complexion is all too clear for all to see.
And look, what this Portia said about you:
'A gentle riddance. Draw the curtains, go.
Let all of his complexion choose me so.'
It's all in this letter from this Launcelot.

MOROCCO
Look, how news of trickery follows us
Even to this place, even here in Trieste,
Where we have come to regain some peace
Some tranquility, some form of sanity,
To recover from our defeated venture,
And heal the sinews of our wounded hearts.
All that glisters is not gold, the inscription
Read, and by God this Portia, this paragon
Of beauty, has proved to be gilded brass,
Naught but a painted face, a mask of lies,
Who rewarded my time, trouble, and expense
With a dead man's skull. Fie! Lady of Belmont!
Is that what I deserve? A dead man's skull?

ARRAGON
And I chose the silver casket, and what
Did I deserve? A fool's head to match mine.

MOROCCO
This woman, Arragon, deserves a ring
Around her beauteous and delicate neck.

ARRAGON
This letter further says she had a lover,
One Bassanio, a habitual bankrupt,
And she had a scheme to prove us fools
While feigning to fulfil her father's wishes.

MOROCCO
By Allah, my scimitar's growing hot
Minute by minute, thirsting for her blood,
To quench my ever seething fury.
My love for thee, Portia, has gone sour,
Has turned to poison and will prove lethal.

ARRAGON
Prince of Morocco, why is it you sought
A Christian woman, one that feeds on pork,
Crabmeat, and bends her knees to images?

MOROCCO
A good question, Prince of Arragon.
Upon wedding her, I meant to show her
The one and only true religion, Islam,
And Prophet Muhammad, peace be upon him.

ARRAGON
And what if she chose to refuse this offer
Of salvation?

MOROCCO
          Then she would refuse
The right way to paradise and its angels.

ARRAGON
Our promise not to woo another woman,
Is now null and void by this discovery.

MOROCCO
But, man, would you again wish to marry
When you see how deceptive gilded beauty
Has proved to be?

ARRAGON
          Only time will tell.

MOROCCO
And time is passing. We need to act.
Let us compensate this good Launcelot
For the service he has rendered us,
While we debate our next step to address
Portia's deception.

ARRAGON
          With all my heart.
I'll give this good man ten silver coins.

MOROCCO
And my ten will make it twenty.

ARRAGON
Let's put this good news, Morocco, to work,
And we'll strive to bring this vain woman down
From the pinnacle of high and mighty Belmont.

MOROCCO
Although a servant, Launcelot must be

Deserving fully of our generosity.

Exeunt Morocco and Arragon.

*

Scene 7

Venice.
Shylock's mean lodging.

Enter Shylock, Tubal, Sassoon, and Watkins.

SHYLOCK
Welcome to Venice, good Signor Sassoon,
And to my home, which is now a mean lodging
Compared to the house I once possessed.

SASSOON
Thank you for your warm welcome, Shylock.
The Duke and Senators of Venice
Have agreed to reexamine your case.

SHYLOCK
But what good would that do for me, Signior,
Again to go through the trickeries of court
And its humbug proceedings?

SASSOON
            Be content.
This time no deceptions will be permitted.
I will be there to make sure this doesn't happen.

TUBAL
This good man has come all the way from London
To argue your case and reclaim your rights.

SASSOON
A grave injustice has been done to you,
And I and Watkins here, my good colleague,
Will seek to vindicate you in court.

WATKINS
We are here to help you, sir.

SHYLOCK
Let me bethink all this. I am too old
To go through the charade of a court trial.

TUBAL
Shylock, there is no time to think things over.
You must gather strength, and with God's help,
Defeat your foes and reclaim your rights.

SHYLOCK
You say so? So be it. What must I do?

SASSOON
Be ready to answer questions in court,
Should the Duke and Senators ask questions.
I'm informed thoroughly with the details
Of your case, thanks to good court records
And the information Tubal has given.
The court will issue summons and subpoenas
To key persons in the first trial. Be ready.

SHYLOCK
So be it, Signior Sassoon. I thank thee
With all my heart, and God guide your plans.

SASSOON
We'll pray for it. Have a good day, Shylock.

Exeunt all.

ACT THREE

Scene 1

The Court in Venice.

     Enter the Duke, Senators, Court Clerk, Sassoon and Watkins. Shylock, Portia and other key persons in the trial wait inside. Tubal, a Moorish girl holding a babe, her parents and relatives, wait on the side. Launcelot waits outside. Venetian citizens at separate doors.

DUKE
I call upon the court clerk to record
All transactions in this trial.

COURT CLERK
     Your Grace,
All transactions will be faithfully recorded.

DUKE
This court has been informed that new evidence
Has emerged in Shylock's trial of last year.
We are obliged to reopen his case.
We have here Signior Sassoon from London
Who, at the request of the Jews of Venice,
Has been lawfully appointed by them

To act as defence lawyer.
We expect to see this hard evidence,
Or else I will forthwith dismiss this court.

SASSOON
Your lordship, the world expects no less
Than what you have just so nobly expressed.
The reputation of Venice is at stake.

DUKE [To court clerk.]
Are all parties in the first trial present?

COURT CLERK
All present, except Antonio, your Grace.

SASSOON
Antonio, whom I wished to confer with,
Has not been seen for the last two days.
As of now, his whereabouts is not known.

DUKE [Consults with the Senators.]
His presence is not crucial to this trial.
We can surely proceed without him.

SASSOON
Definitely, your lordship.

DUKE
Proceed then, Signior.

SASSOON
I call Portia of Belmont to step forward.

[Portia steps forward to face the court.]

DUKE
Are you Portia of Belmont.

PORTIA
Yes, my lord. I am she.

DUKE
You are warned to tell the truth in this court.
Not to do so incurs severe penalties.

PORTIA
I will tell the truth.

DUKE
You may have representation, if you wish.
A state lawyer is ready for the task.

PORTIA
I am capable of defending myself.

BASSANIO
Typical arrogance!

GRATIANO
That blinking idiot, Arragon, was a perfect match for her.

DUKE
Proceed then, Signior Sassoon.

SASSOON
Who is Doctor Bellario?

PORTIA
Bellario is the doctor of law in Padua.

SASSOON
He is also your cousin, isn't he?

PORTIA
Yes.

SASSOON
When the Duke in the first trial had sought
His assistance in the case, he received
A letter from him saying he was sick.

PORTIA
The letter said 'very sick'.

SASSOON
'Very sick'. I thank you for the correction.
Was he really so sick, or did you urge
Cousin Bellario not to come to court?

PORTIA
Signior, I reject your insinuation
That I myself had tampered with the trial.

SASSOON
Temper! Temper! No need to get mad.

DUKE
Signior Sassoon, the witness has a point,
Unless you have evidence to produce.

SASSOON
I humbly withdraw the question, your Grace.

DUKE
So be it.

SASSOON
Now tell us, Portia, who is Balthazar?

PORTIA
Balthazar is a young lawyer of Rome
Recommended by Doctor Bellario
As his substitute in the first trial.

SASSOON
Quite right. Is this Balthazar present here?

PORTIA
As far as I can tell, he is not present.

DUKE
Attendants, see if Balthazar is present.
I know the young man and would recognise
Him at a glance.

NERISSA [Aside.]
        No, you wouldn't, you old fool.

AN ATTENDANT [Searches.]
There is no one here by that name, your Grace.

SASSOON
Of course there is no Balthazar in here.

This will be clear to court in a minute.
I now call on Shylock to come forward.

[Shylock steps forward.]

DUKE
Shylock, I remember you, your bond,
Antonio's forfeiture, and the pound of flesh.
A retrial of your case has been determined
To be necessary.

SHYLOCK
          I thank your lordship
For putting my case under close scrutiny.
Balthazar harangued me on the quality
Of mercy, while meaning to lynch me.
I now let my lawyer defend my rights.

DUKE
Shylock, to err is human, and no court
Is infallible. Judgements handed down
Are always revised, given new evidence.

SASSOON
I call on Watkins, my worthy assistant,
To come forward.

[Watkins, holding a bag, steps forward.]

Go ahead, Watkins.

[Watkins opens the bag and takes out a lawyer's
garment and wig.]

NERISSA
Poor Portia, she has turned pale and frail.
We are both undone. I feel faint myself.

GRATIANO
What a devil of a Jew is this Sassoon!

JESSICA
His assistant is Christian.

LORENZO
May the ground open up and snatch them both.

SASSOON
Portia, you are to wear the lawyer's garment.

PORTIA
I am not a lawyer. I will not do so.

DUKE
Do as Signior Sassoon tells you.
The court orders you to do so.

[Portia puts on the lawyer's garment and hat.]

SASSOON
Your Grace and honourable Senators,
You're about to see a wily impostor,
Decked up in her finery and confident,
Exposed here before your very eyes.
My colleague will now add some embellishments
To conjure up that young lawyer she played
On the stage of this respected court.

FIRST SENATOR
Is this a court of law or a pantomime?

SECOND SENATOR
He better show us a good reason for this.

> [Watkins adds some faint moustache to
> Portia's face.]

DUKE [Stands up in dismay.]
Good Lord, this is the same young Balthazar
Who spoke so eloquently in defence
Of Antonio and the need for mercy!

FIRST SENATOR
Fie, fie, she turned out to be a deceiver.

FIRST CITIZEN
It was a fake trial last time.

SECOND CITIZEN
Show her Christian mercy and hang her.

THIRD CITIZEN
Off with her pretty head.

CLERK
Order in the court!

PORTIA
Your Grace, I admit it was deception.

DUKE
What? Deception, and you admit it too?

PORTIA
But it was made to save Antonio's life
When this Shylock, a foreigner, whetted his knife
To kill one of our Venetian citizens
And spill Christian blood on this very floor.

SASSOON
Your Grace, and distinguished Senators,
Shylock had no intent to kill anyone.
He sought redress not only for the forfeiture
Of the bond but for centuries of abuse.
He felt his own personal agony, yes,
But also that of his own nation.
Years of unmerciful wrong, loss of all
That was dear to him turned into a moment
Of madness, of seeking revenge; a moment
Of madness to which none of us is immune.
And while Shylock suffered a moment
Of madness, Portia, in the name of mercy
Stripped this man not only of his assets
But also of his human dignity,
And she did it, deliberate, in cold blood.
I ask you, then, to think well of Shylock,
As a man of faith, for he is such a man.
And remember what the Psalmist says:
No soul is blameless in the sight of God.
Furthermore, your Holy Scripture is clear
As to the rights of resident aliens.
Aliens have equal rights in the eyes of the law.

[The Duke confers with his Senators.]

PORTIA
Let him cite chapter and verse.

SUNDRY CITIZENS [Shouting.]
Chapter and verse! Chapter and verse!

DUKE
Well, Signior Sassoon, how about chapter and verse?

SASSOON
Does the court have a copy of Scripture?

DUKE [To court clerk.]
Clerk, do we have a copy of Scripture?

CLERK
My lord, we have none. We don't use it here.

SASSOON
Your lordship, no court in England can function
Without a copy of Scripture at the ready.
Watkins, hand me the Holy Scripture.

> [Watkins takes out a Bible from his bag and
> hands it to Sassoon.]

'Thou shalt not pervert the justice of the alien.'
Deuteronomy chapter 24, verse 17.

> [Sassoon offers the opened Bible to the
> Duke to see.]

DUKE [Indicates no need.]
And what is meant by the justice of the alien, Sir.

SASSOON
The Holy Scripture enjoins us not to have
Laws for different classes of people;
Not to have laws for resident aliens,
Different from those for citizens.
All are equal in the eyes of the law.
And I remind the court of Ruth the Moabite,
A foreigner who was treated on such terms.
Shylock has been living and working here
For years. He is as good as a citizen,
Serving the welfare of the community,
Albeit much maligned by fools and bigots.

FIRST SENATOR
Very well answered, Signior.

SECOND SENATOR
Thank you for reminding us of Scripture.
Trade has made us oblivious to its laws.

DUKE [Nodding his consent.]
Let us not forget, and let it be known:
This is a court of law for all people.
Venice is home to diverse nationalities,
And its reputation for justice and truth
Must be guarded and remain beyond blemish.
Neglecting this aim would much impeach
Our system of universal justice for all.

PORTIA
I beg for mercy, though I know I little
Deserve it.

JESSICA [Aside.]
          No, you don't deserve it, witch!

DUKE
Deception in court for a good cause, lady?
Would Cato's daughter descend to this depth
Of brazen felony?

FIRST SENATOR
          Can deceiving Venice
Be right under some circumstance? I think not.

SASSOON
Your lordships, this woman did not only fool
This court but also fooled the laws of Venice,
For she did not act as an impartial lawyer
But as a crafty prosecutor and judge,
Serving in sole defence of Antonio.
Shylock was left in the claws of this fox,
Who in fact sliced off a pound of flesh
From the corpus of Venetian legal system.

DUKE
Impartiality in court is a prerequisite,
And we have erred regarding this matter.

SECOND SENATOR
Yeh, yeh! We fully agree with the Duke.

PORTIA
My lord, I do again beg for mercy.

DUKE
She begs for mercy. What have you to say
To this woman, Shylock. You may speak.

SHYLOCK [Steps forward and confronts Portia.]
Mercy? What mercy? Speak not the word.
Your lordship, this fake Doctor Balthazar,
Who claimed to be a Doctor of Laws,
Was nothing but a Doctor of Lies.
She defended Antonio, who called me dog.

[To Portia.]

Oh what a perfect example you are
Of beauty and the beast in one body.
'Tarry Jew'. Remember? Well, Christian,
Here you will get the justice you deserve.

PORTIA
You're having your day in court, Jew.

SHYLOCK
I have a name. My name is Shylock.

FIRST CITIZEN
She's a racist!

SUNDRY CITIZENS
Racist! Racist! Portia's racist!

FOURTH CITIZEN
Show Jewish quality of mercy, Shylock.

SHYLOCK
The quality of mercy has been soiled,
Stained and spoiled by this painted woman,
For while she was preaching mercy,
She was scheming my own destruction.
She claims she deceived the court to save
A life, the life of one who had, on many
Occasions spat and cursed me for no reason
Other than that I am a Hebrew, strong
In my faith, the faith of our father Abram.
And all for use of that which is mine own.
But as I myself daily ask God for His mercy.
I ask this good court to give this lady
Of quality some quality mercy.

FIFTH CITIZEN
Portia, your god was a Jew!

SIXTH CITIZEN
Shylock, we are with you!

            [Shylock steps back to his place.]

DUKE
Portia of Belmont:
You are under arrest! Guards, handcuff her
And take her to this corner over here.
Myself and my two distinguished Senators
Will deliberate her sentence shortly.

SASSOON
Your Grace, I have more questions for her.
Her complete testimony will determine
The punishment that will fit her crimes.

DUKE
As you wish. Proceed.

SASSOON
Portia of Belmont, what has a signed bond,
A legal contract, to do with mercy?
If you signed and notarized a bond,
Wouldn't you comply with its terms, good or bad?

[Portia takes time to answer.]

Your lordship, the felon ignores my question.

DUKE
Answer the question.

PORTIA
In Antonio's case, the terms were quite fatal.

SASSOON
But he had consented to those harsh terms,
And was more than willing to die for them.
Shylock had the right to exact the penalty,
Isn't that so?

PORTIA
Yes.

SASSOON
Your answer is in the affirmative.

DUKE
Is your answer in the affirmative?

PORTIA
Yes, your Grace, but the whole thing was done
As a jest, in merriment, not in earnest.

DUKE
A notary's seal cannot be a jest.

SASSOON
Tell us, Portia of Belmont, what constitutes
A pound of flesh, human or animal?

PORTIA
I don't understand. What are you driving at?

SASSOON
You warned my good client here last time that
In taking a pound of flesh from Antonio,
He was not to shed one drop of blood.
What did you mean by that? Come, tell us.
Since it is common knowledge to everyone
That flesh is made of tissues and blood,
It was understood that blood would be shed
And Antonio would die. Do you agree?

PORTIA
All of this is history.

DUKE
Answer the question,
Or I will add contempt of court to your felonies!

PORTIA
To answer his question, I do agree.

SASSOON
I put it to you, Portia of Belmont,
That you are a confirmed impostor;
That you hoodwinked the Duke of Venice
And his distinguished Senators with lies
To save the skin of one of your friends.

FIRST SENATOR
How dare you, woman, treating us like this?
Deceiving us in this ignoble manner?

SECOND SENATOR
Or else our court is but a monkey circus.

[Portia is handcuffed and led to a corner.]

GRATIANO
Christians, prepare to be circumcised.

BASSANIO
And your pricks for Jews to slice off.

SASSOON
Your Grace, I now call on one, Nerissa,
A former maid to Portia of Belmont.

[Nerissa steps forward.]

DUKE
Is your name Nerissa, Portia's maid?

NERISSA
Once upon a time maid to her, your Grace.

DUKE
Do you want a lawyer to defend you?

NERISSA
I need no help. I can defend myself.

SASSOON
Did you or did you not impersonate
A lawyer's clerk in the first trial?

NERISSA
You are making a baseless allegation.

SASSOON
We will test it, then. Here are the mantle
And wig of a lawyer's clerk. Put them on.

[Watkins hands him some articles.]

NERISSA
I will not. I am not a lawyer's clerk.

DUKE
You'll stand in contempt of court if you don't,
With penalties for obstructing justice.

[Nerissa puts on the garments.]

By God, this is the same scrubbed boy
That delighted my sight and ear before.

SASSOON
Precisely, your lordship. What we see here
Is female witchcraft tailored to deceive
This high court of Venice and its citizens,
Making a laughingstock of Venetian justice.

DUKE
Oh how offensive she's now to my sight!

NERISSA
Your Grace, I was only following orders.
Portia of Belmont is the one to blame.

DUKE
We have heard this kind of excuse before.
Men, women, and children have been murdered
Using it. It's clear you deceived this court.
Guards, hand-cuff this scrubbed young woman
And let her stand next to her mate.

SHYLOCK
O upright judge! O learned judge!

GRATIANO
Alas, our Christian Duke has turned Jew!

PORTIA
Bitch! Traitor! Traitor! I'll see you hang.

[A fight erupts between Portia and Nerissa.]

DUKE
Guards, separate those two prisoners.

[Guards proceed to separate Portia and Nerissa.]

COURT CLERK
Your lordship, at the door there is a certain
Prince of Nottingham, wishing to present
A case on behalf of Prince of Morocco
And Prince of Arragon, two suitors who
Had sought Portia's hand in matrimony
Through lottery of caskets and inscriptions,
But claim they were craftily cheated
By the prisoner. He has a sealed letter
To submit to the court.

DUKE
        Let the prince be admitted.

        [Launcelot, flamboyantly dressed, makes a
        showy entrance.]

LAUNCELOT
Your Grace, I present you with a sealed letter
From Morocco and Arragon to the defect
They've been cheated by Portia of Belmont.
They had set on long and costly journeys
To win her in marriage, only to find out
They were bamboozled.

        [Hands the letter to the Duke, who peruses it.]

DUKE
        Bamboozled, you say.
Can these princes prove their claims against Portia?

LAUNCELOT
Will your lordship not take their word for truth?
Isn't this a true Christian court of law?

DUKE
A court of law, sir, examines hard evidence.

LAUNCELOT
Is the evidence they present too soft?

DUKE
As soft as a sponge, Prince of Nut . . . Nut . . .

LAUNCELOT
Nottingham, your lordship—in blessed England.

JESSICA
That voice rings familiar.

SASSOON
Your lordship, this man's an impersonator.
There is no prince of Nottingham in England.

DUKE
Another impersonator! This court
Has turned into a bawdy circus theatre.
Guards, divest this man of his fancy clothes!

        [Guards remove Launcelot's hat and mantle.]

JESSICA
It's Launcelot! The uncircumcised lecher!

SHYLOCK
My old, swinish servant! A Christian prick!
The devil whom I taught the laws of Moses.

LAUNCELOT
My ex-wife once told me a court of law
Is the right place for lubricated lies.

DUKE
You mean fabricated.

LAUNCELOT
Lubricated and fabricated, your lordship.

DUKE
Tell your ex-wife the Duke of Venice
Would like to lock her up in a rat hole.

LAUNCELOT
I have no objection to that, your lordship.
A rat hole is the right place for a rat.
But why can't I act a prince for an hour?

DUKE
You have had your act already, sir.

SASSOON
If I may, your Grace, I have information
Touching the lottery. Shylock's daughter,
Jessica, once a friend of Portia, swears

Nerissa had told her of a wily scheme
To doctor the lottery so that Bassanio,
Whom she had long doted on, would win her.

DUKE
Jessica to step forward, if she's present.

      [Jessica steps forward.]

You must tell the truth in this court of law.

JESSICA
With all my heart, I will, your Grace.

SASSOON
Did Nerissa tell you Portia's lottery
Was doctored by her?

JESSICA
      Yes, she did, sir.

NERISSA
She is lying! She is a faithless Jew!

DUKE
Silence!

NERISSA
It's her word against mine.

SASSOON
      Your word is nothing
Since you had purposely deceived this court.

DUKE
The court accepts Jessica's evidence.
Portia, did you bamboozle those princes
By telling Bassanio what casket to choose?

PORTIA
I confess I did, your Grace. Those two princes
Made me feel sick to think any one of them
Could share my kitchen and my bed.
Prince of Arragon is an arrogant ass,
While Prince of Morocco's complexion
Made my hair stand on end and my skin creep.

DUKE
Strange it is your father had left the choice
Of husband to the hazard of lottery.
What father would thus foolishly gamble
On the happiness of his beloved daughter?
Still, you disregarded your father's wishes.

PORTIA
I am indeed forsworn for disobeying
My father's last wishes. I chose to do so,
For I loathed to hazard my virginity
To blind chance. Yet my choice for husband
Alas, has turned out to be blind chance.

DUKE
And so, you brazenly cheated your father
And you cheated this court with your lies.
What an excuse from a lady of quality!
Your beauty has filled you with vanity
And turned you into an unfeeling brute.

What do those princes seek? Speak up, man.

LAUNCELOT
They seek damages, your Grace, not only
For the time, trouble, and travel expenses,
But also for the dignity of being cheated.
Moreover, they urge and deplore you
To lock her up in a dark and smelly dungeon
To intone for her misdeeds and cruelty.

DUKE
We will consider the matter, assess
And impose damages, if necessary.

[To court clerk.]

Any other business?

CLERK
Your lordship, here is a signed petition by
Portia, Nerissa, and Jessica to annul
Their marriages, claiming they've broken down.

SHYLOCK
Oh Jessica, come back to your father!
Repent and return to your ancient faith!

DUKE [Reading the petition.]
This is not a divorce court but I hereby
Make an exception in light of the ugly
And loathsome facts that have herein emerged.
Bassanio, Gratiano and Lorenzo:
Your marriages have indeed broken down,

Beyond any possible repair. Your wives
Seek divorce from each of you. What's your answer?
One speak for all.

BASSANIO [Consulting Gratiano and Lorenzo.]
        We consent to divorce.

DUKE
I have heard you all loud and clear.
Your wives' petition is hereby granted.
All three marriages are now null and void.
Clerk, see that divorce papers are drafted and signed.

CLERK
Yes, your lordship.

DUKE
The court will now adjourn for a short recess.
Myself and the Senators will debate
All issues herein discussed and pass judgements
Pertaining to each defendant.

                Exeunt Duke and Senators.

BASSANIO
I'm glad to divorce you, Portia of Belmont.
You are a vain and empty-headed woman.

PORTIA
A fake lover and a bankrupt husband
That has now despoiled my coffers!

BASSANIO
My coffers! Remember, you have given me
Your Belmont house and all your liquid assets.

PORTIA
'Whoever chooseth me must give and hazard all he hath'
The inscription said, and you had nothing
To hazard but that loan of three thousand ducats
Which you squandered on fine clothes and liveries.

GRATIANO
I say, let Nerissa go to the wind.

NERISSA
What a wild animal you turned out to be!

LORENZO
And may the devil take the Jewess I married!

SHYLOCK
These be the Christian husbands and wives!
They would devour each other alive.

FIRST CITIZEN
Last year's verdicts were unjust.

SECOND CITIZEN
Let's see what becomes of this one.

Re-enter The Duke and Senators.

CLERK
Silence in the court!

DUKE
Myself and these two distinguished Senators
Have briefly debated the punishments
To be meted out. The sundry felonies
That have been committed are quite clear,
And so are the judgements we now give.
First, Portia. Step forward!

[Portia is led by a guard.]

DUKE
We must deal severely with perversion
Of justice. For deceitful impersonation
Of Balthazar and for your lying in court,
We sentence you to one year in prison.

PORTIA
No! Oh no! Show some mercy!

DUKE
Justice, to be fair, must precede mercy.
Mercy without justice would prove foul—
An empty sentiment in the sight of God.
Take her aside. Next, Nerissa. Step forward!

[Nerissa is led by a guard.]

DUKE
For impersonation and lying in court,
Albeit of lesser severity than that
Of your mistress: seven months in prison.

NERISSA
Too harsh, but I accept the sentence.

DUKE
Not that harsh. Take her aside.
Next, our nutty prince. Step forward!

LAUNCELOT
Most obediently, sir.

DUKE
For playing the court jester in this court,
We sentence you to one month in prison.
For Morocco and Arragon, no damages
Are assessed, for as the lottery inscription
Had it: they got as much as they deserved.
Signior Sassoon?

SASSOON
Your Grace, I am here also representing
The case of the Moorish girl who was made
Pregnant by this man. I request the court
To consider the needs of the mother and child.

SUNDRY CITIZENS
Lecher! Lecher! Lecher!

CLERK
Order! Order!

DUKE
Launcelot, are you the father of the Moor's child?

LAUNCELOT
I am not. I am a Christian, your Grace,
And would never opulate with a Moor,
Were she Princess of Morocco herself.

MOORISH GIRL [Holding infant.]
Liar, liar, liar!

HER FATHER
Give us justice, fair Duke!

HER MOTHER
We ask for justice.

DUKE [Consulting with his Senators.]
Let's take a look at the child. Approach!
The boy has a striking resemblance
To his father here. Let us hope he will not
Like his father become a court jester.
The court orders you, Launcelot, to give
A one-time payment of five hundred ducats
Or twenty ducats, monthly, for ten years,
In support of both mother and child.

LAUNCELOT
I am penniless and no longer employed.
Portia and Bassanio have dismissed me.

DUKE
I understand you worked for Shylock once.
Perhaps he'll have pity and take you back.

SHYLOCK
Your lordship:
This man, a sloth and glutton, called me devil.
He is a fool. I will not take him back.
Still, I will find the means to provide
For the mother and child, once I hear
Your decision regarding my own case.

DUKE
Here it is then, Shylock: the court annuls
The deed of gift we had previously issued
In which Lorenzo and Jessica inherit
One half of your wealth upon your death.
The other half, which went to the State,
Will be compensated with half of the assets
Held by Portia of Belmont.

PORTIA
Alas, I have ceded all my possessions
To Bassanio here, who has squandered most
Of my liquid assets. He was, your lordship,
A bankrupt to whom no Christian would lend
Money and had to seek it from a Jew.

DUKE [Consulting with the Senators.]
What you ceded is but a private matter
Between yourself and your former lover.
The court has assessed six thousand ducats
To go to Shylock, plus half the estimated
Value of the Belmont house, which will go
For auction to the highest bidder.

CITIZENS
A wise judge, a wise judge!

TUBAL
A Daniel of a wise judge!

SASSOON
Your Grace, I've investigated the matter
Of forced conversion and discovered that,
Under church rules, it is strictly forbidden,
Albeit it has been practised against Jews.

DUKE
This has been an oversight on our part.
The court accepts your findings in this matter
And we now allow Shylock to go back
To his faith, if he so wishes. Conversion
Was the idea of merchant Antonio.

SHYLOCK
O Moses, Moses, God's sacred laws
Have triumphed at last! Justice is done.
Your Grace, I will provide for this mother
And her dear child, according to their needs.
That much Jewish charity will I show.

DUKE
Clerk, see that documents are drawn, signed
And sealed. All judgements must be enforced.
Our law officers will see to this.
Guards, conduct those felons to prison.
The court wishes you, Shylock, all the best.
I hope you are now truly content.

SHYLOCK
Your lordship, I am content and happy.

        Enter a Messenger [who hands Sassoon a note.]

SASSOON [Opens the note to see what it says.]
Your Grace, here's a note written by Antonio.
I was led to it through my inquiries.

[Sassoon hands the note to the Duke.]

DUKE [Reads the note aloud.]
To him that chances to read this note: I, Antonio a merchant
in Venice have decided to end my life. Since the sea has
taken my ships and all my wealth, it is fitting that it takes
my body too.
                      Antonio

This is sad news. A most foolish act.

        Exeunt Duke and Senators.

BASSANIO
What a fool, what a fool! Poor, Antonio!

        Exit Bassanio.

TUBAL
Antonio the sodomite.

JESSICA
There is room enough for him in hell.

SHYLOCK
God's hand is written large all over it.
My vow, which I had pledged, has come to pass.

SASSOON
You stood for judgement, and this time you won it.
You have had your bond at last, Shylock.

TUBAL
And God did it exacting full interest.

SHYLOCK
Not a single drop of blood has been shed,
As this wicked witch of Belmont enforced.
He drowned himself, the Christian hog,
Even he who spat on me and reviled
Our sacred nation, without an iota
Of mercy, without a speck of charity.

TUBAL
His flesh will be food for fish.

SHYLOCK
          Or bait fish withal.

JESSICA
Father, I kneel and beg your forgiveness.
I repent me of my foolish deeds, the acts
Of a foolish girl. Take me back, father!

SHYLOCK
With all my heart and soul, my daughter.
Oh Jessica, darling, how happy I am!

JESSICA
And here's my mother's turquoise ring. Look, father.
I had the money from the insane Lorenzo
Who squandered his ducats left and right,
Money given to him by Bassanio.
I travelled to Genoa with the monkey
I had purchased, and offered twice its price.
Don't cry, father. Please, please, don't cry.

SHYLOCK
My tears are tears of happiness and joy.
Oh my dearest Jessica. How I rejoice
In your repentance, more than I glory
In this ring. Welcome back to our faith,
The faith of Moses, our master and lawgiver.
In heaven your mother rejoices too.

　　　　Enter a Messenger [who hands Tubal a note and leaves.]

TUBAL
Hear this, Shylock, our synagogue is making
A feast in celebration of your good fortune.

SHYLOCK
Signior Sassoon, will you feast with us?

TUBAL
Please do. It will give us great pleasure.

SASSOON
We must head back to London. A week
In Venice is enough for us and we have
Enjoyed your generous hospitality.

WATKINS
Professor Sassoon is too humble to tell you
He has other knotted cases for him to solve.

TUBAL
We understand, good Signior. Your wages
Will be most generous and sent to you in London.

SASSOON
I have been amply rewarded by seeing
Justice done and truth triumphed at last.
I and my good friend and colleague, Watkins,
Wish you and the Jews of Venice the best
Of wishes. Fare you well.

SHYLOCK and TUBAL
May God guide you safely back to London.

JESSICA
Signior Sassoon, no words can express
My gratitude for defending my father.
Your wide reputation does not speak
Sufficiently high of your fine qualities.

SASSOON
Take good care of your father, Jessica.

JESSICA
I will. I promise.

SASSOON and WATKINS
Our best wishes to you all.

Exeunt Sassoon and Watkins.

TUBAL
And I must to our synagogue ahead of you.
The rabbis and our community expect you,
With flowers, song and dance.

Exit Tubal.

SHYLOCK
        Will be there anon.
On such a day the daughters of Israel
Went out, singing and dancing, with tambourines
Welcoming warriors.

JESSICA
        On such a day
Moses parted the Red Sea and set freedom
From slavery rolling, while the Israelites
Marched with an uplifted arm.

SHYLOCK
        On such a day
Saul killed the Philistines by the thousands
And David, by his ten thousands.

JESSICA
        On such a day
The Jews of Susa celebrated
Queen Esther's victory over Haman.

SHYLOCK
On such a glorious and happy day

Judas Maccabeus defeated Antiochus,
And rededicated the Temple.

JESSICA
Let's go to synagogue, father, and pray.
Let us offer alms to those in need,
And charity to the poor.

SHYLOCK
Like King David, I will sing God's praises
For he has fulfilled my vows to the full.

Exeunt all.

The End

CPSIA information can be obtained at www.ICGtesting.com
Printed in the USA
LVOW051048180812

294878LV00001B/389/P